Anthony Benezet

Mighty Destroyer Displayed

In Some Account of the Dreadful Havock Made by the Mistaken Use

Anthony Benezet

Mighty Destroyer Displayed
In Some Account of the Dreadful Havock Made by the Mistaken Use

ISBN/EAN: 9783744738415

Printed in Europe, USA, Canada, Australia, Japan

Cover: Foto ©ninafisch / pixelio.de

More available books at **www.hansebooks.com**

THE

MIGHTY DESTROYER

DISPLAYED,

IN SOME ACCOUNT OF THE

Dreadful HAVOCK made by the mistaken USE as
well as ABUSE of

DISTILLED SPIRITUOUS LIQUORS.

Anthony

BY A LOVER OF MANKIND.

ECCLESIASTES vii. 29.

*Lo this only have I found, that God hath made man up-
right ; but they have sought out many inventions.*

PHILADELPHIA:

Printed by JOSEPH CRUKSHANK, between Second
and Third Streets, in Market-Street.

M,DCC,LXXIV,

THE

MIGHTY DESTROYER

DISPLAYED, &c.

OBSERVING fome years ago the dreadful havock made by the exceffive ufe of diftilled fpirituous liquors in this part of the world, I was induced to infert in one of the almanacks an extract of what had been written on that fubject by Dr. Hales, fellow of the Royal Society, containing his own remarks, with the fentiments of feveral perfons of note in the phyfical way; whofe knowledge of the nature of diftilled liquors, as well as of their effects on the human frame, beft qualified them to give a right judgment thereon. And as the exceffive and indeed miftaken ufe of thefe liquors continues, and rather increafes, on this Continent, 'tis thought a republication of thofe fenti-

A 2 ments,

ments, with fome additions, may, thro'
divine blefling, be beneficial to many;
particularly to fome well-minded people,
who are under miftaken prejudices on this
moft interefting fubject. " My principal
and indeed only motive," fays this benevolent author, " is to endeavour to roufe
" the caution and indignation of man-
" kind, againft thofe mighty deftroy-
" ers and debafers of the human fpecies,
" *fermented diftilled fpirituous liquors;* thofe
" worfe than infernal fpirits, which bewitch
" and infatuate the nations with their for-
" ceries."—An evil fo amazingly great,
that did not woeful experience too fully
prove it, it feems incredible, that any
whom it concerns could poffibly be fo neg-
ligent, as not to ufe their utmoft endeavours to fupprefs this deftructive *man-
bane.*

That eminent phyfician Dr. Hoffman
exprefly cautions againft the ufe of diftilled fpirituous liquors. " Becaufe," fays
he, " they are, above all things, moft un-
" wholefome, being cauftic burning fpi-
" rits; which, by inflaming the folids, and
" thickening the fluids, caufe obftructi-
" ons, which bring on many fatal dif-
" eafes, fuch as hectick fevers, jaundices,
" dropfies, &c. whereby multitudes are
" yearly and daily deftroyed." He alfo
obferves,

obferves, " that they rot the entrails, fuch
" as the liver, ftomach and bowels ; as
. " it is evident, not only by opening the
" bodies of thofe who are killed by drink-
" ing them, but alfo by what is obferved
" in Germany of the effect which the
" cauftic, fiery, remaining wafh of the di-
" ftillers, has on the guts of hogs ; which
" are thereby fo tendered, that they can-
" not make puddings with them."—He
farther obferves, " That the flefh of fuch
" hogs will not keep, even when falted, .
" fo well as the flefh of other hogs." Dr.
Cheyne, in his effay of health and long
life, fays, " All people, who have any re-
" gard to their health and lives, ought
" to tremble at the firft cravings for fuch
" poifonous liquors. The maladies begot
" by them, bring forth neceffity upon ne-
" ceffity of drams and gills ; till, at laft,
" a kind dropfy, nervous convulfion, flux,
" if not a fever, or phrenzy, fets the poor
" foul free. It has often raifed in me the
" moft melancholly reflections, to fee the
" virtuous and fenfible, bound in fuch
" chains and fetters, as nothing lefs than
" omnipotent grace or the unrelenting
" grave could releafe them from."
Doctor Short, in his hiftory of mineral
waters, page 225. fays, " The oftner I
" reflect on the mifchief done by diftilled
" fpirits,

" fpirits, the more I am confirmed, that
" the human race had been happier had
" drams never been known : and I can-
" not help cordially joining with Doctor
" Allen, in his Synopfis Medici, A.
" 1633. *That the plentiful devouring of thofe*
" *fpirits has killed as many thoufands of*
" *men, as there are ftars in the fky. Nay,*
" *ten times ten thoufands have died by thefe,*
" *more than all the reft of the poifons what-*
" *ever.*"

Doctor Lind, in his treatife on the fcur-
vy, fays, " He obferved moft deftructive
" diftempers to be much increafed, even
" to mortality, by diftilled fpirituous li-
" quors; which failors are too apt gree-
" dily to fwallow down." And Doctor
Hales obferves, from the remarks made
to him by an eminent furgeon, " That
" the ftomachs of great dram-drinkers
" were contracted into half the common
" natural fize, and hard; fomewhat like
" leather, that had been held to the fire.
" The confequence of which was, lofs of
" appetite, and a wafting confumption."

It is pretended, that drams comfort,
warm, and defend from the feverity of
weather, to which men are fometimes expofed; without which, they fay, they
fhould perifh with cold; which is probably, in a great meafure, true of thofe
who

who are habituated to drink them; the blood of such being thereby so much impoverished, that it is well known many of the drinkers of drams are cold and lifeless in the midst of summer, without frequent repetitions: this is what some of them have owned. But on the other hand, how much more able are sober persons to endure cold and hardships? their vital heat not being extinguished by intemperance, does, by its kindly genial warmth, more effectually secure them from the inclemency of the weather, than the false flush of a dram. Besides, it is well known, that men did not perish in the coldest countries for want of drams formerly, when they were not to be had. Of the undoubted truth of this, Captain Ellis gives a full proof in the account of his voyage to Hudson's Bay, page 199. Where he observes, " That the natives on " the very cold coast, of that Bay, to " whom the French are kinder than to " sell distilled spirituous liquors, are tall, " hardy, robust and active; whereas those " of them that are supplied with drams " from the English, are a meagre, dwarf- " ish, indolent people, hardly equal to the " severity of the country, and subject to " many disorders."

And

And as to the pernicious effects of fpirituous liquors in very hot climates, (as on
the coaſt of Guinea) it is obſerved, th
the French and Portuguefe, who do
indulge in diſtilled fpirits, are healthy
compared with the Engliſh; who, drinking freely of fpirits, &c. die faſt. Thus,
alfo, it is obſerved of the women in the
Weſt-Indies, that being fober, they live
long; but it is often otherwife with the
men, who are more generally intemperate.

The unhappy dram-drinkers are fo abfolutely bound in flavery to thefe infernal
fpirits, that they feem to have loſt the
power of delivering themfelves from this
worſt of bondage. How much then is it
the bounden duty of thofe, who have it
in their power, to with-hold this deſtructive *man-bane*, either as parents, maſters,
or rulers to the people committed to their
truſt.

Since then the evil is become fo noto-
riouſly epidemical as to debilitate and de-
ſtroy multitudes, in moſt parts of the
world; it behoves all, who have any bowels of pity for their fellow-creatures, more
eſpecially the governors of the nations,
as guardians and tender fathers, to guard
the people committed to their charge from
this *mighty deſtroyer*. Can there be any
confi-

confideration, of fufficient weight, to the contrary. Is it found policy to encourage *ce in the people, becaufe a prefent re-* nue arifes from their debaucheries? Where will the revenue be, when the people, who fhould pay them, are deftroyed? Are not a hardy, induftrious healthy people, always found to be the moft able to contribute amply to the fupport of government? And will not temperance, in the end, be found a more effectual means to increafe the real wealth and ftrength of a nation, than to make drunkennefs the cheapeft of vices? But if the confideration of the inhumanity of being inftrumental to the deftruction of multitudes, and in a manner, in fome parts of the world, of whole nations, is not of weight enough to influence; yet, fure, the awful confideration, that it muft needs be highly difpleafing to our merciful Creator, to have his favourite creature man thus debafed, difgraced, and deftroyed both in body and foul, ought to have its due weight. Can it in reafon be expected, that he will always remain an unconcerned fpectator of fuch aftonifhing proceedings? And will he not in mercy vifit the nations for thefe things, to prevent the ftill much greater ruin of future generations, in conformity to his ufual

B   method

method of proceeding, when irregularities are arrived to great excesses? This disease has now attained to so enormous a pitch, that it is much to be feared nothing less than God's severe fatherly correction, will effectually cure it in many of the nations; who seem as supine and unconcerned about it, as if only so many thousands of locusts were destroyed thereby: for if in fifty or sixty years this destructive pest has spread thus far and wide, how vastly greater will the havock amongst mankind be in an hundred years more, if some check be not put to its career?

. If it had been said, an hundred years ago, to any of the rulers of the nations, that they should patiently, and even unconcernedly, see such multitudes of their subjects destroyed both body and soul, and that only for filthy lucre; would they not, with indignation, have said as Hazael did to Elisha, 2 Kings viii. 13. " *But* " *what is thy servant a dog, that he should* " *do this great thing?*" The plain truth is, that it is with the nations as it frequently happens to private persons, that when they grow gradually from bad to worse, they, at the same time, become more and more hardened, so as to be even reconciled to practices for which they had

at

at firft the utmoft deteftation and abhor-
rence; for familiarity takes away our attention, and robs things of their power
to ftrike ftrongly upon us.

Though thoufands and tens of thoufands perifh every year by diftilled fpirituous liquors, yet few appear to lay it
effectually to heart. I muft here except the
heads of the poor wild Indians, of the Six
Nations fituate back of New-York, and
other parts of North-America, who being
fenfible of the great deftruction made a-
mongft them by diftilled fpirituous liquors, have long fince, and do ftill continue, earneftly to defire, that no fuch fpirit
fhould be fold to their people. At a treaty
held at Carlifle in this province, with the
deputies of the Six Nations, the Dela-
wares and other weftern Indians, in the
year 1753, Scarrooyady, one of the chiefs
of the Six Nations, fpeaking on behalf of
all the Indians prefent, expreffed himfelf
to the following effect, *viz.* " The rum
" ruins us: we beg you would prevent
" its coming in fuch quantities, by regu-
" lating the traders. We never under-
" ftood the trade was for whifkey *. We
" defire it may be forbidden, and none
                                   " fold

* A fpirit made of grain.

" fold in the Indian country; but that if
" the Indians will have any, they may go
" amongſt the inhabitants, and deal with
" them for it. When theſe whiſkey tra-
" ders come, they bring thirty or forty
" cags, puts them down before us, and
" make us drink, and get all the ſkins
" that ſhould go to pay the debts we
" have contracted, for goods bought of
" the fair trader ; and by theſe means,
" we not only ruin ourſelves, but them
" too. Theſe wicked whiſkey ſellers,
" when they have once got the Indians
" in liquor, make them ſell their very
" clothes from their backs. In ſhort, if
" this practice be continued, we muſt be
" inevitably ruined. We moſt earneſtly,
" therefore, beſeech you to remedy it."
The Indian ſpeaker gave, as is uſual with
them in matters of moment, a treble ſtring
of wampum, in confirmation of this re-
queſt. The deſtructive effect of diſtilled
ſpirits, have alſo extended their baneful
influence amongſt the people of Africa.
It is, in a great meaſure, through the introduction of thoſe infernal ſpirits, that
the poor negroes have been as it were
bewitched, and prevailed upon to capti-
vate their unhappy country people, in order to bring them to the European mar-
ket: hence devaſtation, bloodſhed and mi-
ſery

fery have fpread in their land; many thoufands, and hundreds of thoufands, have
been doomed to a miferable thraldom;
and many, very many, brought to a cru-
el and untimely end : innumerable inftances might be mentioned, to confirm
this melancholy truth ; of which I fhall
mention two, *viz.* Andrew Brue, the
noted French factor, who refided fixteen
years in Guinea, tells us, " That, in ge-
" neral, brandy is the beft commodity
" amongft the negroes, as they love it to
" excefs : that it is eafy, from hence, to
" eftimate the vaft profit made by the
" company, when its ftore-houfe is well
" provided with this liquor." And Fran-
cis Moor, the Englifh factor, in his account of Africa, fays, " That it was to
" the king of Barfailly's infatiable thirft
" for brandy, that his fubjects freedom
" and families were in fo precarious a fi-
" tuation," &c. &c.

It is no uncommon thing for habitual
rum-drinkers; when a fit of ficknefs comes
on, which they conclude will be their laft,
to defire to have plenty of rum by them ;
by which means, they continue intoxi-
cated till death : to fo aftonifhing and de-
plorable a fottifh condition have they re-
duced themfelves ! This is a cafe fo calamitous to mankind, that to have a tho-
rough

rough fenfe of it, and yet not to remon-
ftrate, nor earneftly caution againft it, is
certainly as criminal as it is unfriendly
not to warn a blind perfon of a dangerous precipice or pit; yet, alas! how unconcerned are the greateft part of mankind at this moft enormous ruin of multitudes! In trials for life, what diligence
is ufed to find the occafion of the lofs of
one fubject! What care will not a faith-
ful phyfician beftow for the prefervation
of one life! How did the wife Romans
honour him, who faved the life of one
Roman citizen! But in the prefent cafe,
it is not one, nor one hundred, nor one
thoufand, but probably no lefs than a
million that perifh, yearly, by this worft
of plagues. How then dare the governors of nations be unconcerned or filent
in a caufe in which humanity, virtue, and
the real welfare of mankind, both civil
and religious, are fo deeply concerned?
A caufe, which tends not only to the
weakening the faculties, enervating the
bodies of men, but alfo in debafing the
fpecies, and fhortening the lives of multitudes,

But the moft afflictive and dreadful effect of the common ufe of diftilled fpirituous liquors, are, that it not only hight-
ens the paffions of men and depraves their
morals;

morals; but what is infinitely worfe, and ought to be *an awakening* confideration, they become prophane- and abandoned, and to the laft degree regardlefs of their duty to God and man; the feelings of the mind are gradually benumb'd, and an infenfibility to the healing influence of religion enfues.

The Almighty who has fo curioufly wrought our wonderful frame out of the duft, knowing how prone we are to diforder it by irregularities, hath of his tender fatherly care of us, not only implanted in us a ftrong defire of life and felf-prefervation, but has alfo ftrictly warned us to avoid all deftructive irregularities and vices, and to practife thofe virtues which are fo well adapted to our nature, that they have a direct tendency to give health to the foul, as well as marrow to the bones, Prov. cxi. 8. Yet how is this delicate, this curioufly wrought frame, abufed and difordered by repeated irregularities of many kinds, but never before to the enormous degree that it has of late years arrived at by the exceffive abufe of thefe fermented, diftilled fpirituous liquors, which, by their mifchievous effects, feem to claim Satan himfelf for their author. The benevolent author firft mentioned from whofe collection great part of the

the foregoing is collected, obferves, " That
" if any of his readers fhould think the
" fubject is overpreffed, fuch are defired
" to confider that the calamitous urgency
" of the cafe abfolutely requireth the moft
" pathetical expoftulation, to roufe the
" attention and indignation of mankind,
" againft this greateft of all plagues that
" ever befel unhappy man, which is both
" our fin and our moft fevere punifh-
" ment."

Dr. Cheyne farther obferves, " That if
" only the profligate, the fcoundrel, the
" abandoned run into thefe exceffes, it
" were as vain to endeavour to reclaim
" them, as it were to ftop a tempeft, or
" calm a ftorm : But that now the vice
" is become epidemical, fince it has got
" not only among mechanics and tradef-
" men, but among perfons of the bright-
" eft genius, the fineft tafte, and the moft
" accomplifhed parts. And oh! that I
" could (adds the doctor) give my con-
" fcience the lye in not mentioning them,
" even among the firft and leaft fallen
" part of the creation itfelf, and thofe
" of them too, of the moft elegant parts
" and the ftricteft virtue, even of thofe
" who are in other refpects blamelefs.
" Since the cafe is fo, it will not be amifs
" to fhew, to the evidence of a demon-
                          " ftration,

" ſtration, the folly as well as fruitleſſ-
" neſs of ſuch a courſe. A fit of the
" colick, or of the vapours; a family
" misfortune; the death of a child, or of
" a friend, with the aſſiſtance of the nurſe
" or the next neighbour, often gives riſe
" and becomes the weighty cauſes of ſo
" fatal an effect. A little lowneſs requires
" drops, which paſs readily down under
" the notion of phyſic: Drops beget drams,
" and drams beget more drams, till they
" come to be without weight and without
" meaſure—did this bewitching poiſon ac-
" tually cure or relieve them from time
" to time, ſomething might be ſaid to ex-
" tenuate the folly and the frenzy of ſuch
" a courſe, but on the contrary, it height-
" ens and enrages all their ſymptoms and
" ſufferings ever afterwards, excepting
" the few moments immediately after
" taking it down; and every dram be-
" gets the neceſſity of two more to cure
" the ill effects of the firſt, and one mi-
" nute's indulgence they purchaſe with
" many hours of greater pain and miſe-
" ry,' beſides making the malady more
" incurable. Low ſpiritedneſs itſelf is no
" diſeaſe; beſides there are remedies that
" will relieve it ſo long as there is any oil
" remaining in the lamp.—— Exerciſe,
" abſtinence and proper evacuations, with

C " time

" time and patience, will continually
" make it tolerable; very often they will
" perfectly cure. The running into drams
" is giving up the whole at once, for
" neither laudanum nor arfenick will kill
" more certainly, altho' more quickly."

The miftaken ufe and grievous abufe of
rum and other diftilled fpirits, perhaps
in no cafe appear more palpably than at
the time of harveft, a bufinefs which,
under the Mofaic Difpenfation, was particularly enjoined to be carried on with
humiliation and thankfgiving, and ought
by all means, to be obferved as fuch under
the gofpel; but through the abufe of fpirituous liquors, is made an occafion of a
greater abufe of the creature and difhonour
of the Creator; this arifes, in many, from
a miftaken perfuafion that hard labour,
particularly that of the harveft field, cannot be carried on without a quantity of
rum or other diftilled fpirits; and in fupport of this opinion, we are frequently
told of the many people who have died
in the field through extream heat and fatigue, and it is fuppofed that many more
would die, if a plentiful ufe of fpirituous
liquors was not allowed. But this I am
perfuaded is a great miftake, it being much
more likely that the free ufe of rum occafioned the death of thofe people; the
quantity

quantity they had fwallowed down, fend-
ing a greater flow of fpirits into the head
than the ftrength of the body could fupport. Indeed the repeated large quantities
of rum commonly drank during the whole
time of harveft, keeps up the blood in a
continual ferment and fever, in which
ftate people cannot have a proper reftorative fleep; their conftitutions are thereby
enervated, their lives fhortened, and an
unfitnefs for religious impreffions generally prevails.

 Thefe moft folemn and weighty confi-
derations, have induced fome well-minded people to endeavour to lead, by their
examples, their friends and neighbours
into a contrary practice; and under thefe
attempts, experience has made it manifeft,
that very little or no ftrong liquor is neceffary at thofe times; indeed they have
been convinced that the harveft and other
laborious work, can be very well manag-
ed without making ufe of any fpirituous
liquors at all. If fuch labour was carried
on with fteadinefs and proper moderation,
there would certainly be no need of a recruit of ftrength being fought for by that
means; more frequent intervals of reft,
with a little food, oftener allowed the
reapers, and fmall drinks; fuch as molaffes and water made agreeable with a little
cyder,

cyder, fmall beer, or even milk and water, would fully enable them to perform
their work to their employer's fatisfaction
and their own advantage; and the over-
plus wages they would receive, inftead of
the fpirituous liquors ufually given, might
be fufficient to purchafe bread for their
families.

This fober and moderate manner of proceeding was certainly the general practice
in this province, for a confiderable number of years after its firft fettlement, when
but fmall quantities of ftrong liquors, and
often none at all could be procured*. The
people in thofe early times maintained their
health, and were enabled to perform their
labour to fatisfaction. But this did not
long continue, the great call for our pro-
vifions

---

* In a printed oration, not long fince pronounced
by Dr. Rufh, before the Philofophical Society of
this city, we are told at page 65, " Some of you
" may remember the time, and your fathers have
" told thofe of us who do not, when the difeafes of
" Pennfylvania were as few and as fimple as thofe
" of the Indians. The food of the inhabitants was
" then fimple; their only drink was water; their
" appetites were reftrained by labour: religion ex-
" cluded the influence of fickening paffions: private
" hofpitality fupplied the want of public hofpitals:
" nature was their only nurfe: temperance their
" principal phyfician."

vifions brought us into connections with
thofe countries from whence rum was procured ; and the defire of gain has fince in
a progreffive encreafe, induced our traders
to bring us plenty of diftilled fpirits, and
together with them *difeafes and death* in
return for our flour, and other ufeful produce. So early as the year 1728,* we
find the introduction and confumption of
rum had made an amazing progrefs, and
began to roufe the attention of fome of
the confiderate, may I not fay, of the
lovers of their country in that day. And
from the too apparent general ufe, there is

no

---

* Extract from the Pennfylvania Gazette, for the
year 1728. Philadelphia, the 7th of the 11th
month, 1728, we have the following furprizing
tho' authentick account of rum imported in Pennfylvania the laft year.

6 Puncheons,		Which, by computation is
1556 Hogfheads,		224,500 gallons, of which
927 Tierces,		there was exported but 11400
276 Barrels,		gallons.

So that by a modeft computation there *has been*
confumed in one year, at leaft twenty-five thoufand
pounds in rum. This exceffive drinking of rum, as it
has flain its thoufands, is likely to deftroy its ten
thoufands, for by its corrofive and fiery property, it
debauches the ftomach, dries up the radical moif-
ture, poifons the juices, inflames the blood ; un-
fheaths the bowels, debilitates the nerves and ftupi-
fies the brain.

no room to fuppofe but that it has gone on
in an increafed proportion to our numbers;
tho' not now fo eafily afcertained, from
the additional numbers of ports, and va-
rious means of procuring it : Nor ought
we to omit, in fuch accounts, the large
quantities of whifky and other liquors diftilled amongft ourfelves from grain, fruit,
and molaffes, which cannot well be calcu-
lated.

I have heard of feveral thoughtful people who, from a perfuafion that the common method of giving fpirituous liquors
to labourers was exceeding hurtful, have
made it a condition with thofe they have
employed, not to ufe any fpirituous liquors
in their fields; thefe have had their work
performed to good fatisfaction, and without any damage enfuing to their labourers. Nay, where they have remained any
confiderable time with fuch employers,
they have generally acknowledged themfelves fenfible of the benefit arifing from
having thus totally refrained the ufe of
thofe liquors. A particular inftance of
this kind occurred laft fummer, in the
cafe of Jofhua Evans, of Haddonfield;
this confiderate perfon being convinced
that the ufe of rum and other fpirituous
liquors, was extreamly hurtful to the labouring people; more efpecially during
the

the time of harveſt, apprehended it to be
his duty, to become an example in oppo-
ſition to this pernicious cuſtom; and he
concluded to run all riſques of loſs and damage, which might happen to himſelf ·by
the delay of bringing in his harveſt, rather than comply with a cuſtom which he
apprehended to be ſo deſtructive of his
fellow *men*.

He therefore offered ·ſix·pence per day
more than other farmers, to ſuch labourers as were willing to aſſiſt in bringing in
his harveſt, on condition ·that no ſpirituous liquors ſhould be uſed in his fields.
Notwithſtanding the ſingularity of ſuch
a propoſal, a ſufficient number of labourers offered themſelves, to whom he re-
marked, That the hurrying manner in
which the people drove on their labour in
the harveſt field, cauſed an unnatural ferment and heat in their bodies, and of
courſe an exceſſive thirſt enſued, which
often occaſioned their drinking water, or
·ſmall liquors, in ſuch immoderate degree
as to become hurtful and very dangerous,
that this was generally aſſigned as a rea-
ſon for the uſe of ſpirituous liquors:
That, in order to avoid theſe extremes,
he propoſed to lead them himſelf in the
harveſt work, deſiring they would go no
faſter than he did; they acted accordingly,

ly, and his corn was cut down and brought
in as well, if not better, than ever it had
been before; and tho' the people drank
little but water or milk and water, chufing
it rather than cyder and water, or fmall
beer, which they were not ufed to; they
went thro' their bufinefs with fatisfaction
to him and themfelves. This perfon has
purfued the fame courfe with labourers he
has hired for other work; who, tho' accuftomed to fpirituous liquors, after having
ferved him feveral days, have frankly acknowledged they had done very well *without them*, finding themfelves in a better
ftate both of body and mind, than when
they began to work for him.

This is a plain inftance in contradiction
to the common prejudice, that labouring
people cannot with fafety perform their
work without ufing thofe liquors. Several more examples might be inftanced of
fome confiderate people who have made it
a rule not to make any ufe of fpirituous
liquors, either amongft their workmen in
the profecution of their trades, or on their
plantations. To thefe experience has fhewn,
that their people could not only do as well
without it, but found themfelves much
better in health, and well fatisfied in mind.

Several phyficians of eminence have de-
clared themfelves in favour of this fentiment;

ment; amongft others, the celebrated doctor Buchan, in his Domeftic Medicine, or Family Phyfician, a work fo well efteemed as to have been, within thefe two years, twice reprinted in this city. At page 71, of the Englifh edition, he fays, " Many imagine that hard labour could " not be fupported without drinking " ftrong liquors. This, tho' a common, " is a very erroneous notion. Men who " never tafted ftrong liquors are not only " able to endure more fatigue, but alfo " live much longer than thofe who ufe " them daily*. But fuppofe ftrong liquors " did enable a man to do more work, " they muft neverthelefs wafte the pow- " ers of life, and of courfe occafion pre- " mature old age. They keep up a con- " ftant fever, which waftes the fpirits, " heats and inflames the blood, and pre- " difpofes the body to numberlefs difeaf- " es."

At page the fame, the author tells us, " That all intoxicating liquors may be " confidered as poifons. However dif-

D " guifed,

---

* The few of thefe, who notwithftanding their excefs, may have attained to a confiderable age, it is moft reafonable to fuppofe, would have lived much longer, had they been temperate.

" guifed, that is their real character, and
" fooner or later they will have their ef-
" fect." It is a prevailing opinion in favour of drinking fpirituous liquors at harveft, and other hard labour, that it gives
relief by throwing out the fweat. Now,
moderate quantities of any fmall liquor,
even water itfelf, if not drank too cold,
and particularly if fweetned with molafles,
and a little four'd with fome proper acid,
would certainly anfwer the purpofe, without the bad effects which attend the ufe
of fpirits.

It is well known that a pint of good molafles will, in diftillation, afford rather more
than a pint of good proof rum; therefore
muft contain as much, if not more real
ftrength than the fame quantity of rum,
without any of its noxious qualities; being then in the ftate the Almighty firft
formed it, the fiery property fo clothed
and united with the earthy and balfamick
parts, as to caufe it to be quite friendly to
our nature, and not liable to intoxicate;
as the fpirit alone will, when feparated by
diftillation from the other parts.

Small beer or water mixed with fome
of our home-made wines; or, as before
faid, water mixed with a due quantity of
molafles, made agreeably acid, to fuch as
chufe it, by mixing it with a due proportion

tion of cyder, or fome other acid liquor, or even good vinegar*; milk and water, or even water itfelf, if ufed with caution, will anfwer all the purpofes of common drink for labouring people.

Amongft the feveral prejudices in favour of the miftaken ufe of fpirituous liquors, there is none gives it a greater fanction or fupport, than the prevailing opinion, even with perfons of reputation, that what they term a moderate quantity of rum mixed with water, is the beft and fafeft liquor that can be drank; hence confirming it, that fpirit in one form or

---

* We find by hiftory, that the Roman foldiers, in their long marches, often thro' parching deferts, loaded with heavy armour, ufed vinegar and water as the moft fuitable refrefhment, they carried with them two veffels, either of tin or leather, the one filled with water, the other with vinegar. It alfo appears from fcripture, in the cafe of Ruth, when in the harveft field of Boaz, that it was cuftomary to make ufe of vinegar, as a fuitable refrefhment in that labour. Ruth, chap. ii.

I was informed by a perfon who refided fome time with the Indians, that they made a drink with parched corn, which was very agreeable and refrefhing. The corn, after being parched, is pounded and fifted, the mealy part mixed in water, with moláffes or fugar, to this fome proper acid might be added, which would make it yet more agreeable and wholfome.

or other is neceffary. To fuch who have
not been accuftomed, and think they cannot habituate themfelves to drink water,
there may appear to be fome kind of plea
in this argument, efpecially to travellers,
who often meet with beer, cyder, or other
fermented liquors that are dead, hard,
.four, or not properly fermented, which
tend to generate air in the bowels, pro-
ducing colicks, &c. But I believe if thofe
perfons fuffered the weight of the fubject,
and the confequence of the encourage-
ment they thereby give to the ufe of thefe
deftructive fpirits, to take proper place
with them, it might fuggeft the proprie-
ty, if not neceffity, of introducing a more
falutary practice to themfelves and families. That pure fluid (water) which the
benevolent father of the family of mankind points out for general ufe, is fo ana-
logous to the human frame, that except
in a very few cafes, people might with
fafely gradually ufe themfelves to it : And
as to fuch well-difpofed people who ftill
retain a favourable opinion for the ufe of
fpirit mixed with water, ought they not,
even from love to mankind, to endeavour
to refrain from, and example others a-
gainft it, (on account of the prodigious
havock made by the ufe of fpirits) agreeable to the example fet us by the Apoftle

Paul,

Paul, Cor. viii. 13. *If meat make my brother to offend, I will eat no flesh while the world standeth, lest I make my brother to offend;* how much more then ought they to refrain from that which may tend to establish mankind in a practice so generally destructive; more especially when they consider the danger themselves are in, of encreasing the quantity of spirit with their water; as it has been observed, that the use of this mixture is particularly apt, almost imperceptibly, to gain upon those who use it; so that many otherwise good and judicious people, have, unwarily to themselves and others, fallen with the common herd, a sacrifice to this mighty devourer. And where water is met with, as is sometimes the case, which is scarce fit to drink; its vain to think to remove the noxious qualities by mixing it with spirit; for tho' bad water may be made more palatable by mixing spirit with it, yet all the bad qualities of the water will remain, to which will only be superadded the bad qualities of the spirit. There are many ways proposed by which water may be helped without any such additions, as by filtration, thro' porous stones, or thro' an earthen vessel, in the bottom of which there is a quantity of sand, which retains the noxious mixture. Hard water may

may be made foft by boiling, or by being
expofed to the fun and air. Some propofe
mixing water, which is impure, with
loam; this being well ftirred and left to
fettle, the noxious parts will fubfide with
the loam, and the water may be drawn
off clear and fit for ufe.

Dr. Cheyne in his treatife before mentioned, obferves, That without all perad-
venture, water is the primitive original
beverage; as it is the only fimple fluid fit-
ted for diluting, moiftening and cooling—
the ends of drink, appointed by nature,
and happy had it been for the race of mankind, if other mixed and artificial liquors
had never been invented. " It has been an
" agreeable appearance to me, fays this au-
" thor, to obferve with what frefhnefs and
" vigour thofe who, tho' eating freely of
" flefh meat, yet drank nothing but this e-
" lement, have lived in health, indolence,
" and chearfulnefs to a great age. Water
" alone is fufficient and effectual for all the
" purpofes of human want in drink. Strong
" liquors were never defigned for common
" ufe. They were formerly kept in England,
" as other medicines are, in apothecaries
" fhops." Speaking of the effects of wine (a
liquor in general much lefs hurtful than
diftilled fpirits) which he fays to have
been fo much in ufe at the time he wrote,
that

that the better fort of people fcarcely di-
luted their food with any other liquor, he
remarks, " That as natural caufes will al-
" ways produce their proper effects, their
" blood was inflamed into gout, ftone,
" and rheumatifm, raging fevers, pleuri-
" fies, &c. Water is the only diffolvent
" or menftruum, and the moft certain di-
" luter of all bodies proper for food."

Doctor Short, in his difcourfe of the
inward ufe of water, fpeaks much in its
commendation. He fays, we can draw a
very convincing argument of the excellency of water, from the longevity and
healthfulnefs of thofe who at firft had no
better liquor, and the health and ftrength
of body and ferenity of mind of thofe who
at this day have no other common liquor
to drink. Of this the common people
amongft the Highlands of Scotland, are a
fufficient inftance, amongft whom it is no
rarity to find perfons of eighty, ninety, yea
an hundred years of age, as healthy, ftrong,
and nimble, as wine or ale bibbers are at
thirty-fix or forty*. The excellency of
water,

---

* I was informed by a perfon of credit, from his
own obfervations in Scotland, of the ftrength and
hardinefs of the common people there ; and of their
ability

water, the doctor fays, may be argued from the great fuccefs people, otherwife defpicable, have attained over other nations, while they remained content with the product of nature for drink. Of this the Perfian, Grecian, and Roman monarchies are inftances. This was alfo the cafe of our anceftors, the Saxons, Danes, and Normans, whilft their manners remained fimple, and their food and drink fuch as nature had provided, they encreafed to fuch a degree, that their country not being able to contain them, they were obliged to fend out fwarms of people to feek for fettlements in the more fouthern parts of the world; thefe gradually fettled themfelves in the different parts of the Roman empire: But fince thofe Northern Kingdoms have forfaken the wholfome cuftoms of their forefathers, and habituated themfelves to the ufe of ftrong liquors, they are fo enfeebled, and their numbers have fo much decreafed, that many parts of their

---

ability to bear cold and fatigue; tho' the cold is great in winter, and their fupport in fome parts principally, if not wholly when abroad, confined to oatmeal and water; he has feen a fhepherd laid down to reft or fleep on the mountain, without any fhelter, wrapt up in his plaid in cold fnowy weather, fuch as would have froze moft other people.

their own country now remain uncultivated. The rulers eafy under the pecuniary advantages which arife, themfelves enflaved to the practice of drinking to excefs, look without concern on this enormous ruin of multitudes of their fellow men. Thus it is in Ruffia, where a vaft revenue is raifed from diftilled fpirituous liquors, and a multitude of people proportionably large, are deftroyed thereby. Again fays the doctor, " There is a ridiculous maxim " ufed by drinkers, that water makes but " thin blood, not fit for bufinefs—I fay it " is water only that can endue its drinkers " with the ftrongeft bodies and moft robuft " conflitutions, where exercife or labour is " joined with it, fince it beft afiifts the fto- " mach and lungs to reduce the aliments " into the fmalleft particles, that they may " better pafs the ftrainers of the body, which " feparates the nutritious parts of the blood " to be applyed to the fides of the veffels, " and exercife invigorates the fibres and " mufcles ; whereas the rapid motion of the " blood excited by drinking fpirituous li- " quors, can not fail of being prejudicial " to the body, it will caufe the watery parts " to diffipate and the remaining grow thick " and tough, and the event be obftructions, " inflammations, impofthumations, &c.— " and tho' ftrong liquors afford a greater

E   " flow

" flow of fpirit for a fhort time, yet this
" is always followed with as much low-
" nefs of fpirit ; fo that to gain a neceffary
" ftock of fpirits, the perfon is obliged to
" repeat the fame force, till he learns a
" cuftom of drinking drams. In this we
" are confirmed, if we confider the great
" ftrength and hardinefs of poor rufticks
" in many parts of the world, whofe provi-
" fions is moftly vegetable food, and their
" drink water." The doctor adds, " That
" it often happens that perfons of tender,
" weakly, crazy conftitutions, by refrain-
" ing ftrong liquors and accuftoming them-
" felves to drink water, make fhift to fpin
" out many years."

Doctor Cadogan, in his treatife on
the gout, lately printed in this city, tells
us, " That water is the only liquor nature
" knows of, or has provided for all ani-
" mals, and whatfoever nature gives we
" muft depend upon it, is beft and
" fafeft for us ; accordingly we fee that
" when we have committed any excefs or
" miftake of any kind, and fuffer for it,
" 'tis water that relieves. Hence the chief
" good of bath, fpa, and many other me-
" dicinal waters, efpecially to hard drink-
" ers. It is that element that dilutes and
" carries off crudities and indigeftions, &c.
" the mineral virtues they contain may
                              " make

" make them tolerable to the ftomach in
" their paffage, but do, as I believe, little
" more in the body, it is the water that
" cures. Wine was given us as a cordial."

Cheyne fays he has known men of weak
and tender conftitutions, who could neither eat nor digeft upon drinking wine,
who, by drinking at meals common water
heated, have recovered their appetites and
digeftion, &c. have thriven and grown
plump. Speaking of malt liquors, he gives
it as his fentiment, that a weak ftomach
can as readily, and with lefs pain, digeft
pork and peafe foup, as Yorkfhire or Not-
tingham ale : he adds, That they are of fo
glutinous a nature as to make excellent
bird lime, and when fimmered fometime
over a gentle fire, make the moft fticking,
and the beft plafter for old ftrains that
can be contrived. Even the fmall beer that
is commonly drank at London, if it be
not well boiled, very clear, and of a due
age, muft be hurtful to perfons of weak
nerves and flow digeftion.

Doctor Buchan tells us, The great
quantity of vifcid malt liquor drank by
the common people of England, cannot
fail to render the blood fizy and unfit for
circulation, from whence proceed obftructions and inflammations of the lungs.
Thofe who drink ardent fpirits or ftrong
wine,

wine, do not run lefs hazard; thefe liquors heat and inflame the blood, and
tear the tender veffels of the lungs in
pieces.

Doctor Short, page 33, after deferibing
the many diftempers produced by drinking of malt and other fermented liquors,
adds, That feeing conftitutions differ, it
is not to be expected that fpirituous liquors fhould produce all the fame fymp-
toms in one and the fame perfon, yet that
all drinkers have feveral of them; and if
they come not to that height, its becaufe
they afterwards ufe great exercife or hard
labour, with fometimes thin diluting liquors, which prevent their immediate
hurting*.

Its

---

* Doctor Edward Bancroft, in his natural hiftory of Guiana, which includes the colonies of Suri-
nam, Barbices, &c. writes, That the inhabitants
derive no fmall affiftance from the Indians—fome of
whom refide on almoft every plantation.—Thefe Indians however, are debauched by luxury and intemperance, and their manners but ill agree with thofe
of the Indians who have preferved their natural in-
nocence and fimplicity. They are encouraged in
their propenfity to intemperance by the whites, who
freely fupply them with rum, thereby to attach them
more firmly to their fervice, which confiderably im-
pairs their health and diminifhes their numbers.——

Speaking

Its cuftomary, and often neceffary in
the fummer feafon, particularly in after-
noons, for people who are fpent by labour
or application, to have recourfe to fome
kind of refrefhment. This is generally of
two kinds, very different in their nature
and effect, *viz.* The one is a mixture of
fpirituous liquors, as punch, grog, &c. or
fermented liquors, as cyder, beer, &c. The
other is mild and diluting, fuch as tea,
or coffee, &c. The ufe of fpirituous or
fermented liquors, for the reafons already
given, are hurtful and dangerous; more
efpecially, as the forrowful experience of
many within knowledge, has taught that
there is very great danger of even fober
peopie

Speaking of the difeafes incident to the country, he
fays, Thefe are as numerous as in other countries,
where they have been augmented by cookery, with
its ftimulating, provocative arts, exciting inordinate
appetites, by multiplying the variety of difhes, which
blended in the ftomach, compofe fuch an incongru-
ous medly, that the digeftive organs cannot poffibly
affimilate the pernicious mafs to wholefome chyle.
Nor has intemperate luxury been confined to this
fingle innovation. *Water*, the natural drink of mankind as of all other animals, is now contaminated by
the mixture of pernicious fpirits, which have poifon-
ed one of the principal bleffings of life. From this
fource are derived thofe tribes of difeafes which op-
prefs humanity.

people who ufe them, with what is termed moderation, becoming habituated and gradually encreafing their ftrength and quantity, till it proves the ruin of them-felves and families.

This caution can fcarcely be too often repeated, as it has been fo frequently the melancholy fituation of perfons, otherwife valuable members of fociety. But the ufe of mild diluting drinks, fuch as coffee, or the feveral forts of teas, either of our own produce or thofe brought from the Indies, may be truly termed innocent and friendly to our natures, and very proper to promote a good perfpiration and recruit our fpirits when diffipated thro' application or labour. And as the ufe of thefe innocent dilutors have not efcaped cenfure, more efpecially from perfons who are attached to the ufe of fpirituous or fermented liquors; it may be agreeable to the reader, to hear the fentiments of doctor Cheyne on the fubject. And here it may be well to remark that thefe ob-fervations were addreffed to the people of England, where the heat not being fo great as in thefe parts, thofe reftorative dilutent drinks are not fo frequently ne-ceffary. A dith or two of coffee, the doctor fays, with a little milk to foften it, in raw or damp weather, or on a wa-
teriſh

terifh and flegmatick ftomach, is not only innocent but a prefent relief.——Tea *,
particularly Green, when light and foften-
ed with a little milk, if neither too ftrong
nor too hot, he looks upon as a very proper dilutent, very fuitable to cleanfe the
alimentary paffages, and wafh of the
fcorbutick and urinous falts : He alfo re-
commends tea made of fliced orange or
lemon, as one of the beft promoters of
digeftion after a full meal, or when people are dry between meals. As to perfons of weak and tender nerves, who find
that upon ufing of thefe drinks with freedom, or in too great quantity, they fall
into lownefs and trembling ; fuch ought
to ufe them with moderation and caution.
   Again we know, fays he, that warm water will moft of any thing, promote and
affift digeftion in perfons of weak ftomachs
and tender nerves ; by this alone I have
feen feveral fuch perfons recover to a mi-
racle, when cold mineral waters, bitters,
cordials, and drams have done rather harm
than good.——Tea is but an infufion in
water of an innocent plant : Innocent, he
fays, becaufe we find by its tafte, it has
                          neither

---

   * The middling priced is efteemed the moft
wholfome.

neither poifonous, deleterious, nor acri-
monious qualities; and we are certain from
its ufe, in the countries it come from †,
(which are larger than Europe) that they
receive no damage from it; but on the
contrary, that it promotes both digeftion
and perfpiration. The arguments for its
relaxing the coats of the ftomach and bowels by its heat, are of no force; for unlefs
it be drank much hotter than the blood,
it can do no hurt that way.——However,
I would advife thofe who drink tea plenti-
fully, not to drink it much hotter than
blood warm, whereby they will receive all
its benefits, and be fecure againft all the
harm it can poffibly do.

Doctor Engelbertus Kæmpfer, phyfician
of the Dutch embaffy to the emperor of
Japan, in his account of that country,
giving a particular account of the growth,
preparation, and ufe of tea; fays, It is
fo common in Japan, that travellers drink
fcarce any thing elfe upon the road.—The
frefh gathered leaves are dried or roafted

over

---

† Chambers in his dictionary of arts and fciences,
tells us, That the Chinefe are always taking tea,
efpecially at meals; it is the chiefeft treat wherewith
they regale their friends. The moft moderate take
it at leaft thrice a-day.

over the fire in an iron pan, and when hot, rolled with the palm of the hand on a matt, till they become curled. They have public roafting houfes built for this very purpofe, and contrived fo that every body may bring their leaves to be roafted. The doctor makes no diftinction between green and bohea; the only difference from his account, arifes from the different time of gathering. The firft, gathered whilft the leaves are tender, has the beft flavour and is moft valuable; the fecond is lefs fo: the laft, gathered when the leaves are full grown is the cheapeft. He gives it as his fentiments, from his obfervations of the effect of tea, that when properly prepared and of a due age, it gently refrethes the animal fpirits, and wonderfully chears and comforts the mind; it opens obftructions, cleanfes the blood, and more particularly removes that tartarous matter which is the efficient caufe of gravelly and gouty diftempers. This he fays it does fo effectually, that he never met with any who was troubled either with the gout or ftone, amongft the tea-drinkers of Japan. He adds that he is wholly of opinion that the ufe of teas would be attended with the fame fuccefs in the like cafes, even in Europe, were it not for an hereditary difpofition, for either of thefe diftempers derived to fome perfons from their ancestors;

anceftors ; and which is frequently che-
rifhed and fomented by a too plentiful ufe
of wine, beer, ftrong liquors and flefh
meats. It appears the ufe of tea meets
with oppofition in the Eaft countries, as
well as amongft ourfelves, from thofe perfons whofe practice contradicts the ufe of
thefe kinds of innocent diluting drinks :
for the doctor remarks, That in Japan the
ufe of tea is very much cried down by
thofe perfons who are lovers of fakki beer,
which is there brewed from rice.

All the good qualities afcribed by the
above mentioned phyficians, to foreign
tea, may be as truly applied to teas made
of our own country produce, fuch as fage,
balm, burnet, faffafrafs, &c. &c. thefe I
am perfuaded would anfwer all, if not
more and better purpofes than the foreign
teas. But I fpare to fay much on this
head at prefent, left by difcouraging the
ufe of any mild diluting drink, (efpecially
one in fuch general ufe, and which fimply
confidered as a diluent, muft be acknowledged a good fubftitute,) any ftrength
fhould be given to the ufe of fpirituous
or fermented liquors in its ftead.

We may alfo make a very good refrefhing drink of the nature of coffee ; from
roafted wheat, barley, rye, or chefnuts,
full as agreeable, wholefome, and nourifh-
ing, if not much more fo than coffee itfelf. Upon

Upon the whole it may be afked, What can be done towards preventing or putting a check to the prodigious havock made by the prefent ufe of fpirituous liquors? To this I fhall reply with the refpectable author firft mentioned. Let fuch lawmakers, governors, and rulers, who 1etain any love and pity for their fellow men; let *thefe* be earneftly requefted ferioufly, and folemnly to confider, whether it is not *their* indifpenfable duty to ufe their utmoft endeavours, that a ftop may be put to this dreadful calamity; let not the apprehenfion of lofs or any prefent inconveniency, deter any from doing their duty in this refpect, becaufe there cannot any inconveniencies poffibly arife from the redrefs of this grievance, which deferves to be named with thofe evils which will be the undoubted confequence of its conti-. nuance. The reafons that have hitherto prevailed to the countenancing of this moft deftructive practice, ought furely to be rejected with fcorn and indignation, when the welfare of fuch vaft numbers are fo deeply concerned. What multitudes of lives would thereby be faved, and what innumerable outrages, as theft, murder, &c. prevented: To rectify which, were an apparently vain and fruitlefs attempt, while drunkennefs is made the cheapeft of all vices. A vice which can no otherwife be

                                                effectually

effectually prevented from raging with its prefent exceffive enormity, and fpreading devaftation all around, but by laying fuch high taxes upon diftilled fpirituous liquors, as well thofe made amongft us, as thofe imported from abroad, as will make the drinking it fufficiently expenfive to put it out of the reach of fo great a number of infatiable drinkers, to ufe it; at leaft in its prefent degree of ftrength.——" Alas, " fays he, how aftonifhing a calamity is " this, depraving the morals and fhorten- " ing and deftroying the lives of fuch " multitudes, probably no lefs than a mil- " lion yearly all over the world——were " but one fourth of this number yearly " deftroyed by raging peftilence, with " what earneft fupplications would man- " kind deprecate fo terrifying and fore an " affliction." How fevere a judgment is it, when God leaves men to be their own fcourgers? with how unrelenting and un- merciful a heart do they execute the moft fevere punifhment upon themfelves!—— Particulars who view this matter in its full importance, will query, What can an individual or private man do in the cafe? To thefe it may be obferved, That as po- pular amendments confift wholly of the actions of individuals, every one who is fincere in his defires, that a remedy may be applied to this mighty evil, muft, to

the

the utmoſt of his power, diſcourage the
encreaſe of ſpirituous liquors either by im-
portation, diſtillation, or otherwiſe, and
not deceive themſelves, or rather ſuffer the
God of this world to deceive them by
means of the ſpecious pretences commonly advanced; ſuch as, That other people
will be active in augmenting the quantity
if they do not; or, That however people
may abuſe themſelves thro' exceſs, yet
what is deemed a moderate quantity, may
lawfully be uſed; but it may eaſily be
ſhewn, that theſe and other arguments
commonly advanced, are vain, tho' plau-
ſible pretences; that the true motive is the
deſire of gain: That every new importer
and diſtiller, (and oh that the vender alſo
may bring his ſituation to the true ba-
lance) becomes a party to the evil; gives
freſh ſtrength to the practice, by holding
out an additional quantity, and of courſe
making it in ſome degree cheaper, at leaſt
eaſier for their fellow men to come at, to
the deſtruction of their brethren, children
of the ſame father, and who as chriſtians
they profeſs to love as themſelves.

And as for ſuch who, tho' convinced of
the impropriety of the practice, yet for
fear of not having their labour performed,
or for other reaſons, cannot prevail upon
themſelves to refrain giving it to their ſer-
vants and labourers, let theſe at leaſt ſo
weaken

weaken and qualify it, as to prevent its immediate destructive effects.

A very eminent phyfician has given the following direction for the benefit of thofe who have not wifdom enough left at once to abandon the odious and pernicious practice of drinking diftilled fpirituous liquors, *viz.* By degrees to mix water with the fpirit; to leffen the quantity every day, and keep to the fame quantity of water, till in about the courfe of a week, nothing of the dram kind be ufed along with the water. By this means the perfon will fuffer no inconveniency, but reap great benefit upon leaving off drams or fpirits, as has been tried by many. If any gnawing be left in the ftomach upon quite leaving it off, a little warm broth, weak tea, or any thing of that kind, will be of fervice. The appetite always increafes in a few days after leaving off drams, unlefs by the too long continuance of them, the tone of the ftomach is deftroyed. And when the ftomach is thus affected, a cup of carduus, camomile tea, wormwood or centaury every morning fafting and every evening, will be found a good remedy.

Some

Some GENERAL MAXIMS, moftly drawn from the foregoing, which as they cannot be too obvioufly held up in the view of the young and inconfiderate, its hoped the obfervant reader will excufe the repetition.

THE great rule of diet is to ftudy fimplicity : Nature delights in the moft plain and fimple food ; and every animal, except man, follows her dictates.

Nothing conduces more to health and long life, than abftinence and plain food, with due labour.

Water alone is fufficient and effectual for all the purpofes of human want in drink : It is the univerfal diffolvent nature has provided, and the moft certain diluter of all bodies proper for food ; quickens the appetite and ftrengthens digeftion moft. Doctor Cheyne and doctor Cadogan.

Strong and fpirituous liquors were never defigned for common ufe : They were formerly kept in England, as other medicines are, in apothecaries fhops : If freely indulged, they become a certain tho' flow poifon. Cheyne.

All intoxicating liquors may be confidered as poifons ; however difguifed, that is their real character, and fooner or later they will have their effect. Doctor Buchan.

Every act of intoxication puts nature to the expence of a fever, in order to difcharge the poifonous draught; when this is repeated almoft every day, it is eafy to forefee the confequence.

Fevers occafioned by drinking, do not always go off in a day, they frequently end in an inflammation of the breaft, liver, or brain, and produce fatal effects.

There is no danger in leaving off drinking ftrong liquors at once, the plea for continuing them being falfe and groundlefs. Cheyne.

Strong liquors do not prevent the mifchiefs of a furfeit,

furfeit, nor carry it off fo fafely as water, tho' they feem to give prefent relief. Cheyne.

Many imagine that hard labour could not be fupported without drinking ftrong liquors. This tho' a common, is a very erroneous opinion : Men who never tafted ftrong liquors, are not only able to endure more fatigue, but alfo live much longer than thofe who ufe them daily. Buchan.

Every thing that has paft the fire, fo that it has had due time to divide and penetrate its parts, as in diftillation, as far as it poffibly can, retains a cauftic corrofive and burning quality ever afterwards.

In the continued diftillation of fpirits, the action of fire is fo ftrong as to reduce them to liquid fire at laft ; which will of themfelves evaporate in vifible flames and fumes. Cheyne.

The great quantity of vifcid malt liquor drank by the common people of England, cannot fail to render the blood fizy and unfit for circulation, from whence proceed obftructions and inflammations of the lungs, &c. Buchan.

Malt liquors (excepting clear fmall beer of due age) are extreamly hurtful to tender and ftudious perfons. Cheyne.

There are few great ale drinkers who are not phthifical, nor is that to be wondered at, confidering the glutinous and almoft indigeftible nature of ftrong ale. Buchan.

Thofe who drink ardent fpirits or ftrong wines do not run lefs hazard ; thefe liquors heat and inflame the blood, and tear the tender veffels of the lungs in pieces. Buchan.

Doctor Cadogan in his late treatife on the gout, fays, He cannot allow him to be ftrictly temperate, who drinks any wine or ftrong liquors at all, unlefs it be medicinally.

T H E   E N D.

www.ingramcontent.com/pod-product-compliance
Lightning Source LLC
Chambersburg PA
CBHW021432090426
42739CB00009B/1463